Letts

11+

Success

for

CEM

English & Verbal Reasoning

Quick
Practice Tests

Quick
Practice Tests

Age 9-10

Faisal
Nasim

Contents

About this book

Familiarisation with 11+ test-style questions is a critical step in preparing your child for the 11+ selection tests. This book gives children lots of opportunities to test themselves in short, manageable bursts, helping to build confidence and improve the chance of test success.

It contains 55 tests designed to build key English and verbal reasoning skills.

- Each test is designed to be completed within a short amount of time. Frequent, short bursts of revision are found to be more productive than lengthier sessions.

- CEM tests often consist of a series of shorter, time-pressured sections so these practice tests will help your child become accustomed to this style of questioning.

- If your child does not complete any of the tests in the allocated time, they may need further practice in that area.

- We recommend your child uses a pencil to complete the tests, so that they can rub out the answers and try again at a later date if necessary.

- Children will need a pencil and a rubber to complete the tests and some spare paper to write longer answers. They will also need to be able to see a clock/watch and should have a quiet place in which to do the tests.

- Answers to every question are provided at the back of the book, with explanations given where appropriate.

- After completing the tests, children should revisit their weaker areas and attempt to improve their scores and timings for those tests.

Download a free progress chart from our website
lettsrevision.co.uk/11+

Comprehension

Read the passage and answer the questions that follow. In each question, circle the letter next to the correct answer.

EXAMPLE

Anne bought some new slippers yesterday. They are red with pretty little bows at the front.

What colour are Anne's new slippers?
A Pink
B Blue
C Purple
(D) Red
E Brown

The following is an extract from 'Charlie and the Chocolate Factory' by Roald Dahl

The one thing he longed for more than anything else was . . . CHOCOLATE.

Walking to school in the mornings, Charlie could see great slabs of chocolate piled up high in the shop windows, and he would stop and stare and press his nose against the glass, his mouth watering like mad. Many times a day, he would see other children taking bars of creamy chocolate out of their pockets and munching them greedily, and that, of course, was pure torture.

Only once a year, on his birthday, did Charlie Bucket ever get to taste a bit of chocolate. The whole family saved up their money for that special occasion, and when the great day arrived, Charlie was always presented with one small chocolate bar to eat all by himself. And each time he received it, on those marvellous birthday mornings, he would place it carefully in a small wooden box that he owned, and treasure it as though it were a bar of solid gold; and for the next few days, he would allow himself only to look at it, but never to touch it. Then at last, when he could stand it no longer, he would peel back a tiny bit of the paper wrapping at one corner to expose a tiny bit of chocolate, and then he would take a tiny nibble – just enough to allow the lovely sweet taste to spread out slowly over his tongue. The next day, he would take another tiny nibble, and so on, and so on. And in this way, Charlie would make his sixpenny bar of birthday chocolate last him for more than a month.

But I haven't yet told you about the one awful thing that tortured little Charlie, the lover of chocolate, more than anything else. This thing, for him, was far, far worse than seeing slabs of chocolate in the shop windows or watching other children munching bars of creamy chocolate right in front of him. It was the most terrible torturing thing you could imagine, and it was this:

In the town itself, actually within sight of the house in which Charlie lived, there was an ENORMOUS CHOCOLATE FACTORY!

Just imagine that!

And it wasn't simply an ordinary enormous chocolate factory, either. It was the largest and most famous in the whole world! It was WONKA'S FACTORY, owned by a man called Mr Willy Wonka, the greatest inventor and maker of chocolates that there has ever been. And what a tremendous, marvellous place it was! It had huge iron gates leading into it, and a high wall surrounding it, and smoke belching from its chimneys, and strange whizzing sounds coming from deep inside it. And outside the walls, for half a mile around in every direction, the air was scented with the heavy rich smell of melting chocolate!

1   What type of word is 'greedily'?

   A   Noun
   B   Adjective
   C   Pronoun
   D   Verb
   E   Adverb

2   How often did Charlie get to taste chocolate?

   A   Daily
   B   Weekly
   C   Fortnightly
   D   Annually
   E   We do not know

3   For how long did Charlie make his chocolate bar last?

   A   Ten minutes
   B   Two hours
   C   Less than a day
   D   More than a month
   E   Forever

4   Why do you think the proximity of the chocolate factory bothered Charlie so much?

   A   Because the factory made a lot of noise
   B   Because the smell was terrible
   C   Because it constantly reminded him of chocolate, which he was not allowed
   D   Because the chocolate was poor quality
   E   Because the factory caused pollution

5   Which word best describes Mr Willy Wonka?

   A   Dull
   B   Famous
   C   Aggressive
   D   Tired
   E   Incapable

6   Which word is a synonym of 'scented'?

   A   Perfumed
   B   Sent
   C   Grounded
   D   Bought
   E   Sensitive

Score: .... / 6

Unnecessary Word

You have 6 minutes to complete this test.

You have 6 questions to complete within the time given.

Each of these sentences is shuffled and contains one unnecessary word. Rearrange each sentence correctly and circle the letter above the unnecessary word from the options given.

EXAMPLE

people too at event were there many to the far

A	B	C	D	E
too	many	to	event	far

(Correct sentence: There were far too many people at the event.)

(1) were to in too box the many pencils there

A	B	C	D	E
were	box	to	pencils	there

(2) tomorrow went market to seven yesterday boys the

A	B	C	D	E
market	tomorrow	seven	boys	yesterday

(3) devoured it gazelle as roared barked lion the the

A	B	C	D	E
devoured	barked	lion	the	roared

(4) girl car the new broken buy wanted to a blue

A	B	C	D	E
a	car	wanted	girl	broken

(5) it eat to is decision easy an certainly make not

A	B	C	D	E
decision	easy	certainly	eat	make

(6) I the my summer to love friends me go to and in seaside

A	B	C	D	E
my	me	go	summer	seaside

Score: .... / 6

In each question, underline the correct word from the three choices provided in bold.

EXAMPLE

There are many different ① <u>ways</u> **way types** to solve this problem.

Galileo

In 1581, Galileo entered the University of Pisa to ① **studious study studies** medicine. Armed

with high intelligence and considerable ② **talent thirsty envy**, he soon became knowledgeable

in many subjects, particularly mathematics and physics. Whilst in Pisa, Galileo was ③ **educated**

seeded exposed to the Aristotelian view of the world, then the ④ **arrogant leading**

prostrate scientific authority and the only one sanctioned by the Roman Catholic Church. At

first, Galileo ⑤ **supported sunned froze** this view, like any other ⑥ **intellectual baker**

people of his time, and was on track to be a university professor. However, due to financial

⑦ **luck difficulties growth**, Galileo had to leave the university in 1585 before

⑧ **supplanting grounding earning** his degree. Galileo continued to study mathematics,

supporting himself ⑨ **on with at** minor teaching ⑩ **positions potions partitions**. During

this time he began his two-decade study on objects in motion and published *The Little Balance*,

⑪ **complicating describing frustrating** the hydrostatic principles of weighing small

quantities, which brought him some ⑫ **famous acclaim revenge**.

Score: .... / 12

7

Odd One Out

You have 4 minutes to complete this test.

You have 10 questions to complete within the time given.

In each question, three of the words are related to one another. Circle the letter under the word that is not linked to the other three.

EXAMPLE

bus	car	truck	foot
A	B	C	(D)

(The other three are types of vehicle.)

①

summer	winter	autumn	July
A	B	C	D

②

above	on	below	sweet
A	B	C	D

③

summarise	plan	sadness	agree
A	B	C	D

④

wheel	license	exhaust	chassis
A	B	C	D

⑤

blackberry	raspberry	lemon	strawberry
A	B	C	D

⑥

suffer	agonise	relax	ache
A	B	C	D

⑦

rugby	tennis	football	ball
A	B	C	D

⑧

leader	believer	adherent	follower
A	B	C	D

⑨

sheep	cow	zebra	goat
A	B	C	D

⑩

metres	grams	millimetres	kilometres
A	B	C	D

Score: .... / 10

Test 5	# Antonyms

You have 3 minutes to complete this test.

You have 10 questions to complete within the time given.

In each question, fill in the missing letters to create an antonym of the word on the left.

EXAMPLE

FULL   E ☒M☐ PTY

---

(1) MAJORITY   ☐INO☐ITY

(2) POSITIVE   NE☐ATI☐E

(3) UNLIKELY   PR☐BA☐LE

(4) HELP   H☐N☐ER

(5) NATURAL   ☐RTIF☐☐IAL

(6) LOCATE   M☐SP☐ACE

(7) CLAIM   ☐B☐NDON

(8) BETTER   W☐RS☐

(9) FAKE   ☐EN☐INE

(10) GUILTY   I☐☐OCE☐T

Score: .... / 10

9

Test	# Missing Letters
6	You have 5 minutes to complete this test.
	You have 15 questions to complete within the time given.

In each question, three letters have been removed from a word. Use the clue to help you complete each word.

EXAMPLE

Synonym of REPLY   **AN** SWE **R**

---

(1) Synonym of ACHIEVE   **ACC** .... **LISH**

(2) Antonym of REPAIR   **DA** .... **E**

(3) Synonym of PART   .... **PONENT**

(4) Antonym of BROAD   **NA** .... **W**

(5) Synonym of WEALTHY   **AFFLU** ....

(6) Antonym of RECEIVE   **DO** .... **E**

(7) Synonym of COPY   **I** .... **ATE**

(8) Antonym of SILENT   **AUDI** ....

(9) Synonym of WATCH   **OB** .... **VE**

(10) Antonym of COMBINE   .... **ARATE**

(11) Synonym of CLOSE   **INTI** .... **E**

(12) Antonym of ASSIST   **HIN** ....

(13) Synonym of LUCKY   **FOR** .... **ATE**

(14) Antonym of DANGEROUS   .... **MLESS**

(15) Synonym of ACCEPTABLE   **SATIS** .... **TORY**

Score: .... / 15

10

Correct Sentence

You have 6 minutes to complete this test.

You have 12 questions to complete within the time given.

In each question, circle the letter next to the one sentence that contains correct grammar, spelling and punctuation.

EXAMPLE

(A) I gave him two eggs.

B I gave him two of eggs.

C I gave him too eggs.

D I gave him two egg.

① **A** There are many ways to solve this problem.

B Their are many ways to solve this problem.

C There is many ways to solve this problem.

D They're are many ways to solve this problem.

② **A** The man was always borrowing money to his friend.

B The man was always borrowing money against his friend.

C The man was always borrowing money from his freind.

D The man was always borrowing money from his friend.

③ **A** Many of the hottest country are close to the equator.

B Many of the hottest countries are close to the equator.

C Many of the hottest countries are closed to the equator.

D Many of the hottest countries is close to the equator.

④ **A** You must eat eeither wheat nor dairy if you are allergic to them.

B You must eat neither wheat nor dairy if you are allergic to it.

C You must eat neither wheat nor dairy if you are allergic to them.

D You must eat neither wheat or dairy if you are allergic to them.

Questions continue on next page

(5) A I asked for the book but he did not lend it to me.

B I asked for the book but he did not borrow it to me.

C I will be asking for the book but he was not being lending it to me.

D I asked for the book but he did not lend me.

(6) A I Ben ate so many sweets, that he felt sick.

B Ben ate so many sweets, that, he felt sick.

C Ben ate so many sweets that, he felt sick.

D Ben ate so many sweets that he felt sick.

(7) A She is better at me at writing.

B She is best than me at writing.

C She is better then me at writing.

D She is better than me at writing.

(8) A Paul enjoyed himself on holiday.

B Sarah enjoyed themselves on holiday.

C Paul enjoyed herself on holiday.

D Sarah enjoyed himself on holiday.

(9) A "Where is my favorite pen?" asked Bob.

B "Where is my favourite pen?" Asked Bob.

C "Where is my favourite pen?" asked Bob.

D "Where is my favourite pen"? asked Bob.

(10) A Whichever works the hardest will win the competition.

B Whoever works the hardest will win the competition.

C Whomever works the hardest will win the competition.

D Whoever works the hardest she will win the competition.

(11) A My father impressed the importance of honesty on me.

B My father impressed the importance of honesty for me.

C My father impressed the importance of honesty with me.

D My father impressed the importance of honesty by me.

(12) A Always check your bikes' breaks before you start riding.

B Always check your bike's brakes before you start ridding.

C Always check your bike's breaks before you start riding.

D Always check your bike's brakes before you start riding.

Score: .... / 12

In each question, circle the letter next to the word that best completes each sentence.

EXAMPLE

The girl .... home after school.
- **A** to
- **Ⓑ** walked
- **C** prayed
- **D** bowed
- **E** ate

---

① The writer was able to .... his ideas very clearly and concisely.
- **A** produce
- **B** subtract
- **C** convey
- **D** beneath
- **E** capable

② You must not .... your duty to your fellow students.
- **A** neglect
- **B** aggress
- **C** brave
- **D** persevere
- **E** munch

③ The actor had amassed fame and .... due to his strong performances.
- **A** jokes
- **B** fruit
- **C** obesity
- **D** fortune
- **E** poverty

④ The ruler defeated his enemies and then presided over a period of peace and ....
- **A** turmoil
- **B** mud
- **C** chaos
- **D** prosperity
- **E** piece

Questions continue on next page

(5) The young boy felt shy and .... in front of the cameras.
- **A** assured
- **B** bashful
- **C** confident
- **D** talkative
- **E** extroverted

(6) The worst criminals are placed into .... confinement.
- **A** joyous
- **B** rosy
- **C** flourishing
- **D** majestic
- **E** solitary

(7) A judge must always remain unbiased and ....
- **A** independent
- **B** careless
- **C** partial
- **D** dirty
- **E** racist

(8) The fragrant .... wafted through the building's corridors.
- **A** destruction
- **B** aroma
- **C** ice
- **D** sponge
- **E** hurricane

(9) The men .... the bear and so it reacted angrily.
- **A** praised
- **B** drove
- **C** commended
- **D** taunted
- **E** joked

(10) There are many .... on the path to success.
- **A** encouragement
- **B** denial
- **C** obstacles
- **D** irons
- **E** hole

Score: .... / 10

14

Synonyms

You have 3 minutes to complete this test.

You have 10 questions to complete within the time given.

In each question, fill in the missing letters to create a synonym of the word on the left.

EXAMPLE

NEAR   C[L]OSE

(1) ERRATIC   UN☐RED☐CTABL☐

(2) DUBIOUS   DO☐BTF☐L

(3) UNWILLING   R☐LUCTAN☐

(4) SHY   TI☐ID

(5) VIGOROUS   E☐ERG☐TIC

(6) RELIABLE   ☐EPENDABL☐

(7) PERSISTENT   DE☐E☐MINE☐

(8) CONFUSED   PU☐☐LED

(9) FRAGILE   DE☐ICAT☐

(10) LIVID   O☐TR☐GED

Score: .... / 10

Cloze

You have 5 minutes to complete this test.

You have 12 questions to complete within the time given.

Use the words in the table to fill the gaps in the passage. Each word may be used once only.

EXAMPLE

| feather | curl | shimmered | canopy |

The moonlight .... *shimmered* ....on the surface of the hidden lake.

violent	tumbled	light	uprooted
addressed	bubbling	enormous	flourishing
proudly	contrary	blows	fight

The Oak and the Reeds

Deep within a forest, an (1) .... oak tree towered

(2) .... over the banks of a (3) .... stream.

One evening, a terrible and (4) .... storm descended upon the forest.

The oak was (5) .... by the wind and thrown across the stream. It

(6) .... down among some reeds, which it thus

(7) .... , "I wonder how you, who are so (8) ....

and weak, are not entirely crushed by these strong winds." They replied, "You

(9) .... and contend with the wind, and consequently you are

destroyed; while we, on the (10) .... , bend before the gusts' mighty

(11) .... , and therefore remain (12) ....

and unbroken."

Score: .... / 12

16

You have 3 minutes to complete this test.

You have 10 questions to complete within the time given.

In each question, circle the letter under the word containing a spelling mistake.

EXAMPLE

spread	smear	scarse	scary	seared
A	B	C	D	E

(1)

attack	allow	animate	apprehend	abreviate
A	B	C	D	E

(2)

model	mission	marinayte	mild	musically
A	B	C	D	E

(3)

humour	harass	harbore	herring	hostage
A	B	C	D	E

(4)

vineyard	various	vertical	vaypour	volume
A	B	C	D	E

(5)

ilusion	immediate	illness	impressive	irrigate
A	B	C	D	E

(6)

botched	bezel	brightness	bough	basc
A	B	C	D	E

(7)

lazy	lesiure	lethargic	licence	lopsided
A	B	C	D	E

(8)

convinced	colaborate	curses	crimson	cripple
A	B	C	D	E

(9)

frigid	fallow	former	frantik	formidable
A	B	C	D	E

(10)

orbit	obtuse	organysed	orange	obstinate
A	B	C	D	E

Score: .... / 10

Change a Letter

You have 4 minutes to complete this test.

You have 12 questions to complete within the time given.

In each question, change one letter in the word in capitals to create a new word that matches the definition provided. Write the new word on the line.

EXAMPLE

BAD   A synonym of 'unhappy'   SAD

---

① **CABLE**   A piece of furniture   ....

② **STOCK**   A sudden, upsetting or surprising event   ....

③ **BREAK**   Cold and miserable   ....

④ **COLD**   Brave or courageous   ....

⑤ **HERMIT**   To allow   ....

⑥ **EASY**   Antonym of 'west'   ....

⑦ **GRACE**   A mark indicating the quality of work   ....

⑧ **SHORT**   To bellow or yell   ....

⑨ **POLICE**   A plan of what to do in particular situations   ....

⑩ **PAGE**   To cover with flat stones or bricks   ....

⑪ **HUNGER**   A person who stalks and kills animals for food   ....

⑫ **CHARITY**   The quality of being clear and lucid   ....

Score: .... / 12

Synonyms

In each question, circle the letter above the word that is most similar in meaning to the word given.

EXAMPLE

large

A	B	C	(D)	E
brief	expanse	tiny	huge	lard

(1) strewn

A	B	C	D	E
gathered	shown	allowed	scattered	grown

(2) sweat

A	B	C	D	E
water	sweet	transpire	cooler	perspire

(3) dejected

A	B	C	D	E
subjected	harmed	passive	unhappy	defined

(4) eradicate

A	B	C	D	E
eraser	meaty	destroy	fabricate	passive

(5) spirited

A	B	C	D	E
feisty	whisker	spiritual	bloated	ghost

(6) remote

A	B	C	D	E
television	local	distant	perform	control

(7) alter

A	B	C	D	E
altar	hover	break	change	anger

Score: .... / 7

19

Fill the Letters

In each question, fill in the missing letters to create a correctly spelled word that matches the definition provided.

EXAMPLE

E ☐L☐ b ☐O☐ W   A joint in the arm

① A ☐ CU ☐ ATE   Correct in all details

② S ☐ RA ☐ GE   Unusual or surprising

③ DR ☐ WN   Looking strained from illness

④ ☐ ATTE ☐ N   A repeated decorative design

⑤ R ☐ SE ☐ BLE   To look like or be similar to something

⑥ D ☐ VELO ☐   To advance or grow

⑦ ☐ APAB ☐ E   Able or competent

⑧ F ☐ ONT ☐ ER   A line or border separating two countries

⑨ S ☐ STA ☐ NABL ☐   Able to be maintained at a certain level

⑩ DI ☐ COVE ☐   To find unexpectedly or during a search

Score: .... / 10

Test 15	# Cloze
	You have 5 minutes to complete this test.
	You have 12 questions to complete within the time given.

In each question, write the correct letter in each box to complete the word.

EXAMPLE

A **ra** [i] **n** [b] **ow** is a multicoloured arc that appears in the sky.

The Lion and the Dolphin

(1) **Ro**☐**m**☐**ng** by the seashore, a lion saw a dolphin raise its head above the waves, and

proposed to it that they (2) **c**☐**ntra**☐**t** an alliance, (3) ☐**ug**☐**estin**☐ that of all the

animals they ought to be the best of friends, since one was the king of beasts on the earth, and

the other was the (4) **so**☐**ere**☐**gn** ruler of all the (5) **i**☐**h**☐**b**☐**tants** of the ocean.

The dolphin gladly (6) **c**☐**nse**☐**t**☐**d** to this request. Not long afterwards the lion was

attacked by a wild and (7) **s**☐**va**☐**e** bull, and appealed to the dolphin to aid him. The dolphin,

though quite willing to provide (8) **a**☐☐**ista**☐**ce**, was unable to do so, as he could not by

any means reach the land. Having (9) ☐**an**☐**uish**☐**d** the bull, the lion accused the dolphin

of being a (10) **t**☐**ait**☐**r**. The dolphin replied, "Nay, my friend, don't blame me, but Mother

Nature, who, while (11) **b**☐**es**☐**ing** me with influence over the sea, has quite denied me any

(12) **a**☐**th**☐**rit**☐ on land."

Score: .... / 12

Rearrange the Words

In each question, rearrange the words to create a correct sentence and then write it on the line provided.

EXAMPLE

boy his ate dinner the

The boy ate his dinner.

---

(1) in there sky countless stars the are

....

(2) along blue road the car the whizzed quiet

....

(3) his arsonist fled of the scene the crime

....

(4) retire of this year several decided to my colleagues have

....

(5) it's justify to difficult actions becoming increasingly his

....

(6) a adversary had formidable developed into the politician

....

(7) working watch has out run my because stopped has battery the

....

(8) famine have progress hindered disease country's and the

....

Score: .... / 8

You have 2 minutes to complete this test.

You have 7 questions to complete within the time given.

In each question, circle the letter above the word that is most opposite in meaning to the word given.

EXAMPLE

happy

A	(B)	C	D	E
hippy	sad	calm	up	frozen

(1) convenient

A	B	C	D	E
covert	confused	paradise	prepared	awkward

(2) comply

A	B	C	D	E
disobey	broaden	complicated	fellow	happily

(3) rapt

A	B	C	D	E
stunned	inattentive	tired	wrapped	managed

(4) satisfied

A	B	C	D	E
shallow	hasten	unfulfilled	handy	content

(5) acknowledge

A	B	C	D	E
worsen	wisdom	attribute	ignore	forest

(6) ridiculous

A	B	C	D	E
generous	reasonable	fabulous	grateful	rider

(7) aimless

A	B	C	D	E
amiable	wanderer	focused	bullet	gentle

Score: .... / 7

Comprehension

Read the passage and answer the questions that follow. In each question, circle the letter next to the correct answer.

EXAMPLE

Anne bought some new slippers yesterday. They are red with pretty little bows at the front.

What colour are Anne's new slippers?
A   Pink
B   Blue
C   Purple
D   Red
E   Brown

The following is an extract from 'The Jungle Book' by Rudyard Kipling

Early in the morning Rikki-tikki came to early breakfast in the veranda riding on Teddy's shoulder, and they gave him banana and some boiled egg. He sat on all their laps one after the other, because every well-brought-up mongoose always hopes to be a house mongoose some day and have rooms to run about in; and Rikki-tikki's mother (she used to live in the general's house at Segowlee) had carefully told Rikki what to do if ever he came across white men.

Then Rikki-tikki went out into the garden to see what was to be seen. It was a large garden, only half cultivated, with bushes, as big as summer-houses, of Marshal Niel roses, lime and orange trees, clumps of bamboos, and thickets of high grass. Rikki-tikki licked his lips. "This is a splendid hunting-ground," he said, and his tail grew bottle-brushy at the thought of it, and he scuttled up and down the garden, snuffing here and there till he heard very sorrowful voices in a thorn-bush.

It was Darzee, the Tailorbird, and his wife. They had made a beautiful nest by pulling two big leaves together and stitching them up the edges with fibres, and had filled the hollow with cotton and downy fluff. The nest swayed to and fro, as they sat on the rim and cried.

"What is the matter?" asked Rikki-tikki.

"We are very miserable," said Darzee. "One of our babies fell out of the nest yesterday and Nag ate him."

"Hmm!" said Rikki-tikki, "that is very sad – but I am a stranger here. Who is Nag?"

Darzee and his wife only cowered down in the nest without answering, for from the thick grass at the foot of the bush there came a low hiss – a horrid cold sound that made Rikki-tikki jump back two clear feet. Then inch by inch out of the grass rose up the head and spread hood of Nag, the big black cobra, and he was five feet long from tongue to tail. When he had lifted one-third of himself clear of the ground, he stayed balancing to and fro exactly as a dandelion tuft balances in the wind, and he looked at Rikki-tikki with the wicked snake's eyes that never change their expression, whatever the snake may be thinking of.

"Who is Nag?" said he. "I am Nag. The great God Brahm put his mark upon all our people, when the first cobra spread his hood to keep the sun off Brahm as he slept. Look, and be afraid!"

He spread out his hood more than ever, and Rikki-tikki saw the spectacle-mark on the back of it that looks exactly like the eye part of a hook-and-eye fastening. He was afraid for the minute, but it is impossible for a mongoose to stay frightened for any length of time, and though Rikki-tikki had never met a live cobra before, his mother had fed him on dead ones, and he knew that all a grown mongoose's business in life was to fight and eat snakes. Nag knew that too and, at the bottom of his cold heart, he was afraid.

1 What type of animal was Rikki-tikki?

- **A** Mongoose
- **B** Tailorbird
- **C** Dog
- **D** Cobra
- **E** Tiger

2 Why did Rikki-tikki lick his lips when he went into the garden?

- **A** He was cleaning them
- **B** He was hungry
- **C** He was keeping them moist in the hot sun
- **D** He was excited about hunting in the garden
- **E** He was excited about eating all the roses

3 Why was Darzee upset?

- **A** He could not find his wife
- **B** He was displeased with the arrival of Rikki-tikki
- **C** It was too hot to go outside
- **D** His child had been devoured by Nag
- **E** He could not find anything to eat

4 Which of these words best describes Nag's feelings towards Rikki-tikki?

- **A** Amused
- **B** Amiable
- **C** Polite
- **D** Fearful
- **E** Jealous

5 Which word is a synonym for 'scuttled' as it is used in the passage?

- **A** Froze
- **B** Scampered
- **C** Jumped
- **D** Shuddered
- **E** Ambled

6 What type of word is 'carefully'?

- **A** Adjective
- **B** Noun
- **C** Adverb
- **D** Preposition
- **E** Conjunctive

Score: .... / 6

Unnecessary Word

Test 19	You have 6 minutes to complete this test. You have 6 questions to complete within the time given.	

Each of these sentences is shuffled and contains one unnecessary word. Rearrange each sentence correctly and circle the letter above the unnecessary word from the options given.

EXAMPLE

people too at event were there many to the far

A	B	Ⓒ	D	E
too	many	to	event	far

(Correct sentence: There were far too many people at the event.)

① the over grassy mountains loomed sun the field rocky

A	B	C	D	E
rocky	loomed	over	sun	field

② to soiled to and tend plants their love gardeners herbs

A	B	C	D	E
love	soiled	tend	plants	herbs

③ the shocked the smelled by was disorganisation man's accountant

A	B	C	D	E
shocked	smelled	accountant	was	by

④ that inside house that hoax evil believed it spirits is dwell

A	B	C	D	E
hoax	that	dwell	house	evil

⑤ forest the logging due fast is disappearing to illegal slowly

A	B	C	D	E
the	fast	due	logging	forest

⑥ formed in blue the a pattern sky clouds beautiful the hover

A	B	C	D	E
the	clouds	hover	in	beautiful

Score: .... / 6

26

In each question, underline the correct word from the three choices provided in bold.

EXAMPLE

There are many different (1) <u>ways</u> **way** **types** to solve this problem.

The Marvels of Nature

To our (1) **barbed barbarous barber** ancestors of centuries ago, all was mystery – the thunder,

the rainbow, the growing corn, the ocean and the stars. (2) **Rapidly Frighteningly Gradually**

and by slow steps, they learned to shelter themselves in trees, in (3) **caves seas ceilings**, in huts,

in houses; to find a sure (4) **line treat supply** of food and to provide a stock of (5) **fashionable**

serviceable pretentious clothing. The arts of life were born; tools were invented; the priceless

(6) **blessing bell brisk** of fire was discovered; tribes and clans united for (7) **defense defence**

defamation; some measure of security and comfort was (8) **reignited gambled attained**.

With security and comfort came leisure; and the mind of early Man began curiously to inquire

into the meaning of the mysteries that (9) **distorted mired surrounded** him. That curious

inquiry was the birth of Science. Art was born when some faraway ancestor, in an (10) **lazy idle**

objective hour, scratched on a bone the (11) **likeness frontier taste** of two of his reindeer

fighting, or carved on the walls of his cave the image of the mammoth that he had recently slain

with his spear and (12) **pistol arrows generosity**.

Score: .... / 12

Odd One Out

You have 4 minutes to complete this test.

You have 10 questions to complete within the time given.

In each question, three of the words are related to one another. Circle the letter under the word that is not linked to the other three.

EXAMPLE

bus	car	truck	foot
A	**B**	**C**	**Ⓓ**

(The other three are types of vehicle.)

(1)

salmon	owl	lobster	haddock
A	**B**	**C**	**D**

(2)

shining	glistening	clever	sparkling
A	**B**	**C**	**D**

(3)

book	magazine	newspaper	television
A	**B**	**C**	**D**

(4)

hate	disgusting	admirable	delicious
A	**B**	**C**	**D**

(5)

stool	sofa	window	chair
A	**B**	**C**	**D**

(6)

Italy	Canada	France	Germany
A	**B**	**C**	**D**

(7)

accelerate	whizz	reverse	zoom
A	**B**	**C**	**D**

(8)

dice	cook	cut	slice
A	**B**	**C**	**D**

(9)

forbid	prohibit	outlaw	lounge
A	**B**	**C**	**D**

(10)

garden	herd	flock	school
A	**B**	**C**	**D**

Score: .... / 10

In each question, fill in the missing letters to create an antonym of the word on the left.

EXAMPLE

FULL   E M PTY

1. WEARY   ☐ RE ☐ H

2. DISCARD   A ☐ QUIR ☐

3. DENY   ☐ ONF ☐ SS

4. BACKWARD   SOP ☐ ISTI ☐ ATE ☐

5. PEAK   TRO ☐ GH

6. POWERFUL   INE ☐ FECTIV ☐

7. PREY   P ☐ EDAT ☐ R

8. DIVISION   ☐ ☐ LTI ☐ LICATION

9. RETREAT   A ☐ VAN ☐ E

10. CALCULATED   REC ☐ LES ☐

Score: .... / 10

Missing Letters

You have 5 minutes to complete this test.

You have 15 questions to complete within the time given.

In each question, three letters have been removed from a word. Use the clue to help you complete each word.

EXAMPLE

Synonym of REPLY   AN SWE R

1. Synonym of SLOPPINESS   **CARELE** .... **ESS**

2. Antonym of ABUSE   **C** .... **LIMENT**

3. Synonym of SCURRY   **SCA** .... **R**

4. Antonym of STRAIGHTFORWARD   .... **TERIOUS**

5. Synonym of HARASS   **PES** ....

6. Antonym of ATROCIOUS   **W** .... **ERFUL**

7. Synonym of TRIGGER   **AC** .... **ATE**

8. Antonym of ARREST   **RELE** ....

9. Synonym of DEBUT   **BEG** .... **ING**

10. Antonym of LACK   **S** .... **LUS**

11. Synonym of INTRIGUING   **FASC** .... **TING**

12. Antonym of RESERVED   **OUTG** .... **G**

13. Synonym of CAMOUFLAGED   **DI** .... **ISED**

14. Antonym of VALUABLE   **WORT** .... **SS**

15. Synonym of STARTLE   **SH** ....

Score: .... / 15

Correct Sentence

You have 6 minutes to complete this test.

You have 12 questions to complete within the time given.

In each question, circle the letter next to the one sentence that contains correct grammar, spelling and punctuation.

EXAMPLE

(A) I gave him two eggs.

B I gave him two of eggs.

C I gave him too eggs.

D I gave him two egg.

① **A** We emerged unharmed through the wreckage.

B We emerged unharmed from the wreckage.

C We emerged unharmed with the wreckage.

D We emerged unharmed of the wreckage.

② **A** There were several officers here yesterday.

B There were several officers here tomorrow.

C There are several officers here yesterday.

D There were several officers here yesterday

③ **A** There isnt too much I can do to help you.

B There isn't two much I can do to help you.

C There isn't to much I can do two help you.

D There isn't too much I can do to help you.

④ **A** The teacher asked "How are you all doing today?"

B The teacher asked, "How are you all doing?" today

C The teacher asked, How are you all doing today?"

D The teacher asked, "How are you all doing today?"

Questions continue on next page

(5)
- **A** The queen's reign lasted seven days.
- **B** The queen's rain lasted seven daze.
- **C** The queen's reign lasted seven daze.
- **D** The queen's rain lasted seven days.

(6)
- **A** John asked his friend, who was, called Fred, to help him.
- **B** John asked his friend, who was called Fred to help him.
- **C** John asked his friend, who was called Fred, to help him.
- **D** John asked his friend who were called Fred to help him.

(7)
- **A** The angry old man shouted at my and my friend.
- **B** The angry old man shouted at me and my friend.
- **C** The angry old man shouted at I and my friend.
- **D** The angry old man shouted at my friend and I.

(8)
- **A** The idol young boy eight all the cookies.
- **B** The idle young boy ate all the cookies.
- **C** The idle young boy eight all the cookies.
- **D** The idol young boy ate all the cookies.

(9)
- **A** The bag was full of apples, bananas and oranges.
- **B** The bag was full of apples, bananas and oranges
- **C** The bag was full of apples bananas and oranges.
- **D** The bag was full of apples and bananas and oranges.

(10)
- **A** The man was convicted from stealing the book.
- **B** The man was convicted of stealing the book.
- **C** The man was convicted by stealing the book.
- **D** The man was convinced of stealing the book.

(11)
- **A** Elephants can be found in both Africa and India.
- **B** Elephants can be found in both africa and india.
- **C** Elephants can be found in both Africa and india.
- **D** Elephants can be found in both africa and India.

(12)
- **A** The chancellour held up a colored sheet.
- **B** The chancellor held up a colored sheet.
- **C** The chancellour held up a coloured sheet.
- **D** The chancellor held up a coloured sheet.

Score: .... / 12

Complete the Sentence

In each question, circle the letter next to the word that best completes each sentence.

EXAMPLE

The girl .... home after school.

A   to
(B) walked
C   prayed
D   bowed
E   ate

① My brother loved football so he was .... to watch the match.
  A   floating
  B   disbeliever
  C   aggrieved
  D   excited
  E   common

② The forest's dense foliage made it almost ....
  A   frigid
  B   transparent
  C   wander
  D   impenetrable
  E   happy

③ Rhinos are an .... species as there are very few left in the wild.
  A   deadly
  B   threat
  C   obvious
  D   aquatic
  E   endangered

④ The .... between the two tribes ensured that they would both be safe.
  A   battle
  B   insults
  C   argument
  D   capability
  E   alliance

Questions continue on next page

(5) The family was .... by the hotel manager's rude behaviour.
- **A** quaking
- **B** shocked
- **C** killed
- **D** charmed
- **E** allowed

(6) A gust of wind .... the leaves across the road.
- **A** scattered
- **B** disdained
- **C** organised
- **D** warned
- **E** promoted

(7) The debater failed to win the contest because his arguments were ....
- **A** convincing
- **B** dashing
- **C** trivial
- **D** insightful
- **E** formidable

(8) Your .... driving caused the accident.
- **A** sensible
- **B** hoping
- **C** reckless
- **D** calculated
- **E** defined

(9) The bodyguard .... the minister to his car.
- **A** hid
- **B** froze
- **C** framed
- **D** grew
- **E** escorted

(10) The .... nurse worked extremely hard and cared deeply about her patients.
- **A** lazy
- **B** negative
- **C** wither
- **D** dedicated
- **E** nasty

Score: .... / 10

Synonyms

In each question, fill in the missing letters to create a synonym of the word on the left.

EXAMPLE	
NEAR	c[L]OSE

1. BLATANT — OB☐IOU☐

2. COHESIVE — ☐NIT☐D

3. DELIBERATE — ☐NTE☐TIONA☐

4. LOFTY — ☐OWE☐ING

5. NOVEL — UN☐S☐AL

6. RECTIFY — C☐R☐ECT

7. REVEL — D☐LIGH☐

8. DISPOSE — DIS☐AR☐

9. EXTRACT — ☐IT☐DRAW

10. ERADICATE — ☐LIMINAT☐

Score: .... / 10

Cloze

Use the words in the table to fill the gaps in the passage. Each word may be used once only.

EXAMPLE

| feather | curl | shimmered | canopy |

The moonlight ....*shimmered*............on the surface of the hidden lake.

maximum	paused	afforded	intensely
maintained	arose	shadow	escalated
sought	transport	traveller	claimed

The Camel's Shadow

A traveller hired a camel and its owner to (1) .... him to a distant place.

It was an (2) .... hot day and, with the sun shining at

(3) .... strength, the two men (4) .... to rest.

They both (5) .... shelter from the heat in the

(6) .... of the camel. As this only (7) ....

protection for one, and as the traveller and the owner of the camel both

(8) .... it, a vicious dispute (9) .... between

them. The owner (10) .... that he had only leased the camel and not its

shadow. The (11) .... asserted that he had, with the hire of the camel,

also hired its shadow. The quarrel (12) .... from words to blows, and

while the men fought, the camel escaped and ran off.

Score: .... / 12

36

Spelling Mistake

You have 3 minutes to complete this test.

You have 10 questions to complete within the time given.

In each question, circle the letter under the word containing a spelling mistake.

EXAMPLE

spread	smear	scarse	scary	seared
A	B	Ⓒ	D	E

1

eturnal	ending	ember	effective	enemy
A	B	C	D	E

2

clinch	close	creaiton	covering	caution
A	B	C	D	E

3

dialoge	daisy	dumb	dazed	definite
A	B	C	D	E

4

ponder	painting	plyable	perfect	posture
A	B	C	D	E

5

joiner	jear	javelin	jealousy	joker
A	B	C	D	E

6

woe	win	wel	web	wine
A	B	C	D	E

7

styfle	sounded	stereo	sacrifice	something
A	B	C	D	E

8

evict	energy	effort	eazy	element
A	B	C	D	E

9

broken	bizzare	bounty	brake	bazaar
A	B	C	D	E

10

frantic	forgiveness	focused	finest	felow
A	B	C	D	E

Score: .... / 10

Change a Letter

In each question, change one letter in the word in capitals to create a new word that matches the definition provided. Write the new word on the line.

EXAMPLE

BAD   A synonym of 'unhappy'   *SAD*

①	**FRONT**	Ice crystals that form on the ground	
②	**HOPE**	Extravagant or intensive publicity	
③	**WINNER**	The coldest season of the year	
④	**REIGN**	To pretend	
⑤	**HACK**	A bird of prey	
⑥	**SCARS**	An item of clothing worn when it's chilly	
⑦	**MOVER**	To remain in one place in the air	
⑧	**FAIRY**	Containing or made from milk	
⑨	**COMB**	A prolonged state of deep unconsciousness	
⑩	**SEWER**	To divide by cutting	
⑪	**BATCH**	To carry out a task badly	
⑫	**SLIME**	To carve or segment	

Score: .... / 12

Synonyms

You have 2 minutes to complete this test.

You have 7 questions to complete within the time given.

In each question, circle the letter above the word that is most similar in meaning to the word given.

EXAMPLE

large

A	B	C	Ⓓ	E
brief	expanse	tiny	huge	lard

(1) economical

A	B	C	D	E
aspire	frugal	economy	grovel	alerted

(2) rigorous

A	B	C	D	E
thorough	rig	through	rainy	piled

(3) neglected

A	B	C	D	E
empowered	maintained	governed	derelict	faced

(4) encircle

A	B	C	D	E
angle	trade	surround	waste	leave

(5) nimble

A	B	C	D	E
lazy	neutral	thimble	amazed	quick

(6) reputable

A	B	C	D	E
reputation	crime	notorious	trustworthy	rally

(7) bounded

A	B	C	D	E
restricted	breeze	released	boasted	hatred

Score: .... / 7

Fill the Letters

Test 31	

You have 4 minutes to complete this test.

You have 10 questions to complete within the time given.

In each question, fill in the missing letters to create a correctly spelled word that matches the definition provided.

EXAMPLE

E ☐L☐ B ☐O☐ W   A joint in the arm

1 A ☐ R ☐ PT   Sudden and unexpected

2 ☐ OIS ☐ EROUS   Noisy and energetic

3 M ☐ NDA ☐ E   Lacking interest or excitement

4 PR ☐ SPE ☐ OU ☐   Successful in material terms

5 IN ☐ RE ☐ ID   Fearless or unafraid

6 ☐ ON ☐ RO ☐ ERSY   Prolonged public disagreement

7 ST ☐ ATE ☐ Y   A plan of action to achieve an overall aim

8 C ☐ LA ☐ ITY   An event causing sudden damage or distress

9 D ☐ S ☐ IT ☐ TE   Extremely poor and unable to provide for oneself

10 RE ☐ LENI ☐ H   To fill something up again

Score: .... / 10

40

In each question, write the correct letter in each box to complete the word.

EXAMPLE

A **ra** [i] **n** [b] **ow** is a multicoloured arc that appears in the sky.

King Uther

In the hall of his Roman palace at London, King Uther, Pendragon of the Island of Britain, was

dying. He had been sick for many years and was (1) **f**☐**rc**☐**d** to lie in his bed, (2) **gn**☐**wi**☐**g**

his beard with wrath at his weakness, while the pagan Saxons (3) **ra**☐**ag**☐**d** his territory.

They left in their tracks the smoking ruin of broken towns and (4) ☐**ba**☐**don**☐**d** villages,

where many had perished on the hearths, churches stood pillaged and (5) **d**☐**s**☐**cr**☐**ted**

and priests and nuns (6) ☐**ande**☐**ed** in the wilds.

At length, when the pagans, bold and (7) **in**☐**ole**☐**t**, ventured near London, the king could

not bear his shame and anguish any longer. He (8) **ro**☐**n**☐**ed** up his army and met the

savage pagans at Verulam. After a fierce and (9) **d**☐**struc**☐**ive** battle, he finally managed to

(10) **e**☐**pel** the enemy from his lands.

Following this (11) **e**☐**c**☐**un**☐**er**, the weak king returned to bed and beside him sat the wise

wizard Merlin. On the third night, the king suddenly awoke from his (12) **stu**☐**or** and clutched

Merlin's hand.

Score: .... / 12

Rearrange the Words

In each question, rearrange the words to create a correct sentence and then write it on the line provided.

EXAMPLE

boy his ate dinner the

The boy ate his dinner.

---

(1) attract the was store to struggling shoppers department

....

(2) until new year come not policy the will into next effect

....

(3) complimentary a you we like would to beverage offer

....

(4) the arrogant my concerns dismissed lawyer valid

....

(5) the endorse decided king neither to candidate

....

(6) drink the lowered head stream to the from rhinoceros his

....

(7) was very a mother woman my perceptive

....

(8) toddlers captivated by clown were the magical the

....

Score: .... / 8

Antonyms

In each question, circle the letter above the word that is most opposite in meaning to the word given.

EXAMPLE

happy

A	Ⓑ	C	D	E
hippy	sad	calm	up	frozen

① straight

A	B	C	D	E
crooked	line	strive	strait	paler

② benign

A	B	C	D	E
enemy	hostile	disaster	fraudulent	nine

③ renounce

A	B	C	D	E
upper	announce	dramatic	attack	accept

④ admire

A	B	C	D	E
like	detest	hold	friendship	adhere

⑤ alarming

A	B	C	D	E
clock	watching	frustrating	comforting	arouse

⑥ sluggish

A	B	C	D	E
slither	slug	suffering	brisk	coffee

⑦ serious

A	B	C	D	E
serial	grave	adamant	timely	comical

Score: .... / 7

Comprehension

Read the passage and answer the questions that follow. In each question, circle the letter next to the correct answer.

EXAMPLE

Anne bought some new slippers yesterday. They are red with pretty little bows at the front.

What colour are Anne's new slippers?
A   Pink
B   Blue
C   Purple
D   Red
E   Brown

The following is an extract from 'One Summer: America 1927' by Bill Bryson

On a warm spring evening just before Easter 1927, people who lived in tall buildings in New York were given pause when the wooden scaffolding around the tower of the brand-new Sherry-Netherland Apartment Hotel caught fire and it became evident that the city's firemen lacked any means to get water to such a height.

Crowds flocked to Fifth Avenue to watch the blaze, the biggest the city had seen in years. At thirty-eight storeys, the Sherry-Netherland was the tallest residential building ever erected, and the scaffolding – put there to facilitate the final stages of construction – covered the top fifteen storeys, providing enough wood to make a giant blaze around its summit. From a distance, the building looked rather like a just-struck match. The flames were visible twenty miles away. Up close, the scene was much more dramatic. Sections of burning scaffolding up to fifty feet long fell from a height of five hundred feet and crashed in clattering showers of sparks in the streets below, to the gleeful cries of the spectators and the peril of toiling firemen. Burning embers dropped onto the roofs of neighbouring buildings, setting four of them alight. Firemen trained their hoses on the Sherry-Netherland building, but it was a token gesture since their streams could not rise above the third or fourth storey. Fortunately, the building was unfinished and therefore unoccupied.

People in 1920s America were unusually drawn to spectacle, and by ten o'clock that evening the crowd had grown to an estimated one hundred thousand people – an enormous gathering for a spontaneous event. Seven hundred policemen had to be brought in to keep order. Some wealthy observers, deflected from their evening revels, took rooms in the Plaza Hotel across the street and held impromptu 'fire room parties', according to the New York Times. Mayor Jimmy Walker turned up to have a look and got soaked when he wandered into the path of a hose. A moment later a flaming ten-foot-long plank crashed onto the pavement near him and he accepted advice to withdraw. The fire did extensive damage to the upper reaches of the building but luckily did not spread downward and burned itself out about midnight.

1   In what month could the events of this passage have taken place?
- **A**   January
- **B**   March
- **C**   June
- **D**   October
- **E**   December

2   What is a synonym for the word 'token' as it is used in the passage?
- **A**   Coin
- **B**   Voucher
- **C**   Happy
- **D**   Taken
- **E**   Symbolic

3   How many buildings were set alight in total?
- **A**   One
- **B**   Two
- **C**   Three
- **D**   Four
- **E**   Five

4   Which word best describes the crowd's general attitude to the fire?
- **A**   Entertained
- **B**   Fearful
- **C**   Disgusted
- **D**   Indifferent
- **E**   Horrified

5   What is an antonym for the word 'spontaneous', as it is used in the passage?
- **A**   Happy
- **B**   Planned
- **C**   Depressed
- **D**   Impulsive
- **E**   Fortunate

6   Why did the Mayor decide to leave the scene?
- **A**   He was almost soaked by a hose
- **B**   The crowd were booing him
- **C**   He feared for his safety
- **D**   He was bored
- **E**   He had an urgent meeting

Score: .... / 6

Unnecessary Word

You have 6 minutes to complete this test.

You have 6 questions to complete within the time given.

Each of these sentences is shuffled and contains one unnecessary word. Rearrange each sentence correctly and circle the letter above the unnecessary word from the options given.

EXAMPLE

people too at event were there many to the far

A	B	C	D	E
too	many	to	event	far

(Correct sentence: There were far too many people at the event.)

① the match supporters attended loyal every fragrant

A	B	C	D	E
loyal	fragrant	supporters	match	every

② the correct not of the was answer sure boy biased

A	B	C	D	E
biased	sure	correct	of	answer

③ young confidently her admiringly the seniors teacher challenged

A	B	C	D	E
admiringly	teacher	confidently	young	seniors

④ obstacles stoning there path significant ahead are the in

A	B	C	D	E
there	obstacles	ahead	stoning	path

⑤ seven scenarios for the company were the two troubling both

A	B	C	D	E
troubling	two	for	seven	company

⑥ translation it inaccurate the to the be found scholars

A	B	C	D	E
inaccurate	it	the	found	scholars

Score: .... / 6

In each question, underline the correct word from the three choices provided in bold.

EXAMPLE

There are many different (1) <u>ways</u> way types to solve this problem.

The Lisbon Earthquake

The Lisbon earthquake (1) **suck struck shivered** on the morning of 1 November 1755,

causing serious (2) **relief humour damage** to the port city of Lisbon and killing an estimated

60,000 people. Violent shaking (3) **reinforced demolished renovated** large public buildings

and about 12,000 (4) **articles animals dwellings**. Since 1 November is All Saints' Day, a large

part of the population was (5) **feeling attending weighing** Mass at the moment the earthquake

struck. The churches were (6) **unable unkempt unsure** to withstand the seismic shock and

so they (7) **connived collapsed hurled**, killing or injuring thousands of (8) **spectators**

worshippers guards.

Modern research (9) **denigrates indicates cries** that the main seismic source was the faulting

of the seafloor along the tectonic plate (10) **crossings boundaries journeys** of the mid-Atlantic.

The earthquake (11) **floundered revolutionised generated** a tsunami that produced

(12) **clouds waves winds** about 6 metres high in Lisbon and as high as 20 metres in Cadiz.

Score: .... / 12

Odd One Out

You have 4 minutes to complete this test.

You have 10 questions to complete within the time given.

In each question, three of the words are related to one another. Circle the letter under the word that is not linked to the other three.

EXAMPLE

bus	car	truck	foot
A	B	C	Ⓓ

(The other three are types of vehicle.)

①
knee	elbow	arm	ankle
A	B	C	D

②
oak	leaf	ash	sycamore
A	B	C	D

③
nephew	man	uncle	grandfather
A	B	C	D

④
sometimes	seldom	infrequently	rarely
A	B	C	D

⑤
brush	painting	canvas	paint
A	B	C	D

⑥
pomegranate	strawberry	tomato	cucumber
A	B	C	D

⑦
elephant	snake	lion	zebra
A	B	C	D

⑧
honest	sincere	trustworthy	deceitful
A	B	C	D

⑨
forge	blacksmith	baker	butcher
A	B	C	D

⑩
wood	jungle	ocean	forest
A	B	C	D

Score: .... / 10

Antonyms

You have 3 minutes to complete this test.

You have 10 questions to complete within the time given.

In each question, fill in the missing letters to create an antonym of the word on the left.

EXAMPLE

FULL   E [M] PTY

1. SIMPLIFY   C☐MPL☐CATE

2. TOXIC   H☐ALT☐Y

3. WARY   TR☐STIN☐

4. VILE   PL☐ASA☐T

5. SAVE   S☐U☐NDER

6. BLATANT   SU☐TLE

7. COLOSSAL   ☐IN☐TE

8. ELOQUENT   I☐ARTI☐ULAT☐

9. INSOLENT   ☐OL☐TE

10. RECEDE   ☐☐VANCE

Score: .... / 10

Missing Letters

In each question, three letters have been removed from a word. Use the clue to help you complete each word.

EXAMPLE

Synonym of REPLY **AN** SWE **R**

1. Synonym of EAGER **ENT** .... **IASTIC**

2. Antonym of RIGID **FLEX** .... **E**

3. Synonym of SANCTION .... **HORISE**

4. Antonym of PROTECT **EXP** ....

5. Synonym of YIELD **SU** .... **NDER**

6. Antonym of ELUSIVE **OBT** .... **ABLE**

7. Synonym of ANNUL **IN** .... **IDATE**

8. Antonym of GRIEVE **CELE** .... **TE**

9. Synonym of ENCLOSE .... **ELOP**

10. Antonym of LISTLESS **ANIMA** ....

11. Synonym of VARIABLE **CH** .... **EABLE**

12. Antonym of PASSIONATE **I** .... **FFERENT**

13. Synonym of INCORRECT **E** .... **NEOUS**

14. Antonym of SENSIBLE **UNRE** .... **NABLE**

15. Synonym of AROMATIC **F** .... **RANT**

Score: .... / 15

Correct Sentence

You have 6 minutes to complete this test.

You have 12 questions to complete within the time given.

In each question, circle the letter next to the one sentence that contains correct grammar, spelling and punctuation.

EXAMPLE

Ⓐ I gave him two eggs.

B I gave him two of eggs.

C I gave him too eggs.

D I gave him two egg.

---

① **A** Warm clothing is essential for this voyage.

B Warm clothing is esential for this voyage.

C Warm clothing are essential for this voyage.

D Warm clothing is essential for this voyage

② **A** I forgave him of betraying me.

B I forgave him by betraying me.

C I forgave him in betraying me.

D I forgave him for betraying me.

③ **A** You need to apply for some work experiences

B You need to aply for some work experience.

C You need to apply for some work experience.

D You need to apply for some work experiences.

④ **A** Linda drew seven fish and three sheep on the paper.

B Linda drew seven fishies and three sheep on the paper.

C Linda drew seven fish and three sheeps on the paper.

D Linda drew seven fishies and three sheeps on the paper.

Questions continue on next page

(5) A   Pollution of the environement is a global issue.

     B   Pollution of the environments is a global issue.

     C   Pollution of the environment is a global issue.

     D   Pollution of the environment is an global issue.

(6) A   The couragous girl swiftly defeated the dragon.

     B   The courageous girl swiftly defeated the dragon.

     C   The courageuos girl swiftly defeated the dragon.

     D   The courageous girl swiftl defeated the dragon.

(7) A   Please don't forget to pick up your litter.

     B   Please dont forget to pick up your litter.

     C   Please don't forget to pick up your litters.

     D   Please dont forget to pick up your litters.

(8) A   All accepting one of the caterpillars transformed into butterflies.

     B   All except one of the caterpillar transformed into butterflies.

     C   All except one of the caterpillars transformed into butterflies.

     D   All accept one of the caterpillars transformed into butterflies.

(9) A   "There was no choice!" Yelled the instructor.

     B   "There was no choices!" yelled the instructor.

     C   "There were no choice!" yelled the instructor.

     D   "There was no choice!" yelled the instructor.

(10) A   The astronaut, who had trained for many years, was selected to go into space.

     B   The astronaut who had trained for many years was selected to go into space

     C   The astronaut, who had trained, for many years, was selected to go into space.

     D   The astronaut, who had trained for many years, were selected to go into space.

(11) A   All the children participated in the event.

     B   All the children participated about the event.

     C   All the children participated by the event.

     D   All the children participated on the event.

(12) A   It's warm in summer than in winter.

     B   Its warmer in summer than in winter.

     C   It's warmer in summer than in winter.

     D   It's warmer in summer then in winter.

Score: .... / 12

Complete the Sentence

You have 5 minutes to complete this test.

You have 10 questions to complete within the time given.

In each question, circle the letter next to the word that best completes each sentence.

EXAMPLE

The girl .... home after school.
A   to
B   walked
C   prayed
D   bowed
E   ate

① The scientists used inaccurate data so the results of the study are ....
A   able
B   flawed
C   pure
D   bubbly
E   superlative

② The machine was able to produce parts twice as .... as the workers.
A   biggest
B   longest
C   better
D   fast
E   slower

③ The judge agreed with his colleague's ruling so he .... it.
A   blew
B   rejected
C   massaged
D   smoked
E   upheld

④ Susana loved working with her hands so she looked for a job that involved .... work.
A   calculating
B   manual
C   mental
D   debating
E   timeless

Questions continue on next page

(5) The audience was .... female though there were a few men in the crowd too.
  A   minority
  B   flashy
  C   capable
  D   predominantly
  E   holistic

(6) The .... of water, due to the drought, was beginning to alarm the officials.
  A   prevalence
  B   flood
  C   hope
  D   abundance
  E   lack

(7) The boy studied .... and completed every assignment.
  A   diligently
  B   efficient
  C   haplessly
  D   frustrated
  E   injury

(8) The civilians on both sides of the conflict were suffering and wished for the hostilities to

  ....
  A   enjoy
  B   cease
  C   develop
  D   flourish
  E   progress

(9) The businessman was a tough .... and drove a hard bargain.
  A   trumpet
  B   trivial
  C   crack
  D   negotiator
  E   laugher

(10) The immigrant missed her homeland and .... to return there one day.
  A   dejected
  B   yearned
  C   hope
  D   refused
  E   grew

Score: .... / 10

Synonyms

You have 3 minutes to complete this test.

You have 10 questions to complete within the time given.

In each question, fill in the missing letters to create a synonym of the word on the left.

EXAMPLE

| NEAR | C[L]OSE |

(1) ROUSE   EX□ITE

(2) SAGE   W□SE

(3) VACANT   U□OC□UPI□D

(4) FLOOD   IN□NDA□E

(5) DEDUCTION   SUB□RACTI□N

(6) MALICIOUS   M□LEVOLE□T

(7) DIVULGE   D□SCLOS□

(8) EVICT   □ANISH

(9) JOVIAL   C□EER□UL

(10) CLOUDY   □VERC□ST

Score: .... / 10

55

Cloze

Use the words in the table to fill the gaps in the passage. Each word may be used once only.

EXAMPLE

| feather | curl | shimmered | canopy |

The moonlight ....*shimmered*.......... on the surface of the hidden lake.

spirit	encountered	extremely	fault
yielded	infirmities	blamed	seized
rotten	praised	youth	master

The Hound

A hound, who in the days of his (1) .... and strength had never

(2) .... to any beast of the forest, (3) .... in

his old age a boar in a hunt. He (4) .... him boldly by the ear but could

not retain his hold because his teeth had decayed and become (5) ....

The boar struggled free and fled. The hound's (6) ...., viewing

from afar, was (7) .... disappointed and fiercely scolded the dog.

The hound looked up and said, "It was not my (8) ...., master;

my (9) .... was as good as ever but I could not help my

(10) .... I rather deserve to be (11) .... for

what I have been, than to be (12) .... for what I am."

Score: .... / 12

Spelling Mistake

You have 3 minutes to complete this test.

You have 10 questions to complete within the time given.

In each question, circle the letter under the word containing a spelling mistake.

EXAMPLE

spread	smear	scarse	scary	seared
A	B	C	D	E

1

rally	rewthless	raindrop	renovate	rubbery
A	B	C	D	E

2

seldom	shallow	sidle	synical	savage
A	B	C	D	E

3

colourfull	cable	comb	cutter	cardiac
A	B	C	D	E

4

paradox	powerful	peeved	passionate	plouw
A	B	C	D	E

5

afterthought	ally	arogance	artistic	affectionate
A	B	C	D	E

6

revolution	resourceful	respectful	repetiton	randomised
A	B	C	D	E

7

invigilate	irrigate	internet	industry	intrust
A	B	C	D	E

8

assortment	absolute	alleviate	asail	aggrieved
A	B	C	D	E

9

layman	lounging	lazyness	leverage	levelled
A	B	C	D	E

10

contrast	conseal	connive	convince	contribute
A	B	C	D	E

Score: .... / 10

Change a Letter

You have 4 minutes to complete this test.

You have 12 questions to complete within the time given.

In each question, change one letter in the word in capitals to create a new word that matches the definition provided. Write the new word on the line.

EXAMPLE

BAD   A synonym of 'unhappy'   *SAD*

① **START**   Clever or intelligent   ....

② **FEED**   To pay attention   ....

③ **DEFINE**   To improve or perfect   ....

④ **ATTACK**   To join or fasten things together   ....

⑤ **FAVOUR**   To enjoy to the full   ....

⑥ **BRUISE**   A holiday voyage on a ship   ....

⑦ **SPEAR**   To cut the wool off (a sheep)   ....

⑧ **YAWN**   A young deer   ....

⑨ **SWALLOW**   Superficial or insubstantial   ....

⑩ **PASTE**   The sensation of flavour   ....

⑪ **GLAMOUR**   To shout loudly and insistently   ....

⑫ **WILLOW**   To roll about and lie in mud   ....

Score: .... / 12

Synonyms

You have 2 minutes to complete this test.

You have 7 questions to complete within the time given.

In each question, circle the letter above the word that is most similar in meaning to the word given.

EXAMPLE

large

A	B	C	D	E
brief	expanse	tiny	huge	lard

(1) diminish

A	B	C	D	E
drive	grow	follow	replenish	reduce

(2) overdue

A	B	C	D	E
opportunity	outstanding	agree	remote	over

(3) generate

A	B	C	D	E
general	jealous	juice	frustrate	produce

(4) thwart

A	B	C	D	E
permit	group	frustrate	fraud	free

(5) surly

A	B	C	D	E
surprised	satisfied	soften	jovial	brusque

(6) fuse

A	B	C	D	E
rocket	supreme	combine	neither	destroy

(7) deplete

A	B	C	D	E
freight	drain	understand	aid	fill

Score: .... / 7

Test	**Fill the Letters**
48	You have 4 minutes to complete this test. You have 10 questions to complete within the time given.

In each question, fill in the missing letters to create a correctly spelled word that matches the definition provided.

EXAMPLE

E L B O W   A joint in the arm

① AMP ☐ E   Sufficient or adequate

② R ☐ BB ☐ SH   Waste

③ E ☐ DEAR ☐ NG   Lovable or adorable

④ ☐ M ☐ IVORE   A person that eats both plants and animals

⑤ SE ☐ ENE   Calm or peaceful

⑥ CUL ☐ ☐ BLE   Blameworthy

⑦ ASP ☐ RE   To aim or hope for something

⑧ PL ☐ CA ☐ E   To appease or pacify

⑨ DI ☐ ULG ☐   To reveal or disclose

⑩ ☐ ☐ CTIFY   To correct or repair

Score: .... / 10

Cloze

In each question, write the correct letter in each box to complete the word.

EXAMPLE

A ra⬚i⬚n⬚b⬚ow is a multicoloured arc that appears in the sky.

The History of Mathematics

The area of study commonly known as the history of mathematics is (1) p⬚im⬚ri⬚y

an investigation into the origin of (2) ⬚⬚scover⬚es in the discipline and, to a lesser

extent, an investigation into the mathematical methods and (3) n⬚tati⬚n of the past.

Prior to the modern age and the (4) ⬚orld⬚ide spread of knowledge, written examples

of new mathematical developments have only come to light in a few (5) are⬚s. The most

(6) ⬚nc⬚ent mathematical texts available are Babylonian and Egyptian. These treatises

concern the so-called Pythagorean theorem, which seems to have been the most ancient and

(7) w⬚d⬚spr⬚ad mathematical development after basic arithmetic and geometry.

Greek mathematics greatly refined the methods, especially through the introduction of

(8) d⬚du⬚tive reasoning and rigour in proofs. Chinese mathematics made significant early

(9) c⬚ntri⬚utio⬚s, including a place value system. The Hindu-Arabic numeral system

and the rules for the use of its operations, in use (10) t⬚ro⬚g⬚out the world today,

probably evolved over the course of the first (11) ⬚illenniu⬚ AD in India and were

(12) tr⬚ns⬚it⬚ed to the west via the notable work of Islamic scholars.

Score: .... / 12

Rearrange the Words

You have 8 minutes to complete this test.

You have 8 questions to complete within the time given.

In each question, rearrange the words to create a correct sentence and then write it on the line provided.

EXAMPLE

boy his ate dinner the

The boy ate his dinner.

---

(1) be experiments conduct facility will used new to the

....

(2) still world great many people the in live poverty in

....

(3) army the across battlefield the marched determined

....

(4) allotment in gardener planted his seeds the some

....

(5) do beyond point this proceed not please

....

(6) for goals set impossible team the manager his

....

(7) approval his unanimous with met was proposal new

....

(8) damp left were dry clothes outside to my

....

Score: .... / 8

Antonyms

In each question, circle the letter above the word that is most opposite in meaning to the word given.

EXAMPLE

happy

A	ⒷB	C	D	E
hippy	sad	calm	up	frozen

(1) intervene

A	B	C	D	E
interest	interfere	crime	ignore	hostage

(2) poison

A	B	C	D	E
antidote	venom	pain	snake	avoid

(3) scrupulous

A	B	C	D	E
hound	scalpel	refer	wasteful	careless

(4) exclusive

A	B	C	D	E
allowance	exclusion	festive	joining	common

(5) talented

A	B	C	D	E
boastful	inept	great	skilled	tribe

(6) gather

A	B	C	D	E
scatter	lavish	frosty	gained	crowd

(7) construct

A	B	C	D	E
cane	disappoint	dismantle	torn	build

Score: .... / 7

Comprehension

Read the passage and answer the questions that follow. In each question, circle the letter next to the correct answer.

EXAMPLE

Anne bought some new slippers yesterday. They are red with pretty little bows at the front.

What colour are Anne's new slippers?
A Pink
B Blue
C Purple
D Red
E Brown

The following is an extract from 'The House of Hades' by Rick Riordan

During the third attack, Hazel almost ate a boulder. She was peering into the fog, wondering how it could be so difficult to fly across one stupid mountain range, when the ship's alarm bells sounded.

"Hard to port!" Nico yelled from the foremast of the flying ship.

Back at the helm, Leo yanked the wheel. The Argo II veered left, its aerial oars slashing through the clouds like rows of knives. Hazel made the mistake of looking over the rail. A dark spherical shape hurtled toward her. She thought: Why is the moon coming at us? Then she yelped and hit the deck. The huge rock passed so close overhead it blew her hair out of her face.

CRACK!

The foremast collapsed, sail, spars, and Nico all crashing to the deck. The boulder, roughly the size of a pickup truck, tumbled off into the fog like it had important business elsewhere.

"Nico!" Hazel scrambled over to him as Leo brought the ship level.

"I'm fine," Nico muttered, kicking folds of canvas off his legs.

She helped him up, and they stumbled to the bow. Hazel peeked over more carefully this time. The clouds parted just long enough to reveal the top of the mountain below them: a spearhead of black rock jutting from mossy green slopes. Standing at the summit was a mountain god, one of the *numina montanum*, Jason had called them. Or *ourae*, in Greek. Whatever you called them, they were nasty. Like the others they had faced, this one wore a simple white tunic over skin as rough and dark as basalt. He was about twenty feet tall and extremely muscular, with a flowing white beard, scraggly hair, and a wild look in his eyes, like a crazy hermit. He bellowed something Hazel didn't understand, but it obviously wasn't welcoming. With his bare hands, he pried another chunk of rock from his mountain and began shaping it into a ball.

The scene disappeared in the fog, but when the mountain god bellowed again, other *numina* answered in the distance, their voices echoing through the valleys.

"Stupid rock gods!" Leo yelled from the helm. "That's the third time I've had to replace that mast! You think they grow on trees?"

Nico frowned. "Masts are from trees."

1 Which word is closest in meaning to 'yanked'?
   A   Yelled
   B   Tugged
   C   Broke
   D   Hurried
   E   Ate

2 What was unusual about the Argo II?
   A   It had four masts
   B   It could dive underwater
   C   It was indestructible
   D   The colour of its paint
   E   It was a ship that could fly

3 Which word is not an accurate description of the mountain god?
   A   Tall
   B   Relaxed
   C   Bearded
   D   Dangerous
   E   Powerful

4 Why would Nico need to replace the mast again?
   A   Because it was rotten
   B   Because it was not tall enough
   C   Because it was destroyed
   D   Because it was getting old
   E   We do not know

5 How can we tell that the mountain god was extremely strong?
   A   He had a deep voice
   B   He had a long beard
   C   He captured and destroyed the ship
   D   He could throw boulders the size of pickup trucks
   E   His tunic gave him special powers

6 Which genre best describes the writing in this passage?
   A   Fiction
   B   Poetry
   C   Tragedy
   D   Non-fiction
   E   Romance

Score: .... / 6

Unnecessary Word

You have 6 minutes to complete this test.

You have 6 questions to complete within the time given.

Each of these sentences is shuffled and contains one unnecessary word. Rearrange each sentence correctly and circle the letter above the unnecessary word from the options given.

EXAMPLE

people too at event were there many to the far

A	B	C	D	E
too	many	to	event	far

(Correct sentence: There were far too many people at the event.)

① you to having must teeth brush remember your

A	B	C	D	E
teeth	must	having	your	remember

② another respect growth wrestlers one two the not did

A	B	C	D	E
another	two	not	growth	respect

③ loved evening to in the music the instrument nurse play

A	B	C	D	E
instrument	music	evening	in	play

④ fell coined for the ruse banker the forger's

A	B	C	D	E
ruse	coined	for	banker	fell

⑤ tusk considerate elephants very are and caring

A	B	C	D	E
considerate	elephants	tusk	very	caring

⑥ the salt disappeared horizon the over setting sun

A	B	C	D	E
disappeared	horizon	setting	salt	sun

Score: .... / 6

Spelling Mistake

In each question, circle the letter under the word containing a spelling mistake.

EXAMPLE

spread	smear	scarse	scary	seared
A	B	Ⓒ	D	E

1.

jealous	jovial	jeering	jam	justise
A	B	C	D	E

2.

heroizm	hollow	hover	hopeful	heaven
A	B	C	D	E

3.

brazen	builder	baseless	bussiness	bothered
A	B	C	D	E

4.

cable	comission	cover	calibre	creed
A	B	C	D	E

5.

peeling	pillow	percieve	punishment	prayer
A	B	C	D	E

6.

lever	lanes	liver	longer	lettice
A	B	C	D	E

7.

powerful	proklaim	priority	pint	pointing
A	B	C	D	E

8.

medium	moving	mindful	medle	masterful
A	B	C	D	E

9.

oposite	offering	overtly	opinion	ogre
A	B	C	D	E

10.

initiate	igloo	immersion	interpret	iritate
A	B	C	D	E

Score: .... / 10

Change a Letter

In each question, change one letter in the word in capitals to create a new word that matches the definition provided. Write the new word on the line.

EXAMPLE

| BAD | A synonym of 'unhappy' | *SAD* |

① **TAPE**   A sleeveless cloak   ....

② **OVERT**   To prevent or ward off   ....

③ **COWER**   A sleeve or wrapper   ....

④ **POSTER**   To trouble and annoy   ....

⑤ **AROUND**   The solid surface of the earth   ....

⑥ **HERD**   A plant used to flavour food   ....

⑦ **LEARN**   To long for or crave   ....

⑧ **CRANKED**   Split or broken   ....

⑨ **SPINDLE**   To defraud or deceive   ....

⑩ **SLIVER**   To tremble and quiver   ....

⑪ **LAZY**   Vague or ill-defined   ....

⑫ **WATER**   To provide what is needed or required   ....

Score: .... / 12

Answers

Test 1 Comprehension

Q1 *E*

Adverb

Q2 *D*

Annually

Q3 *D*

More than a month

Q4 *C*

Because it constantly reminded him of chocolate, which he was not allowed

Q5 *B*

Famous

Q6 *A*

Perfumed

Test 2 Unnecessary Word

Q1 *C* *to*

Correct sentence: There were too many pencils in the box.

Q2 *B* *tomorrow*

Correct sentence: Seven boys went to the market yesterday. OR Yesterday seven boys went to the market.

Q3 *B* *barked*

Correct sentence: The lion roared as it devoured the gazelle.

Q4 *E* *broken*

Correct sentence: The girl wanted to buy a new blue car.

Q5 *D* *eat*

Correct sentence: It is certainly not an easy decision to make.

Q6 *B* *me*

Correct sentence: My friends and I love to go to the seaside in summer. OR In summer my friends and I love to go to the seaside.

Test 3 Cloze

Q1 *study*

Q2 *talent*

Q3 *exposed*

Q4 *leading*

Q5 *supported*

Q6 *intellectual*

Q7 *difficulties*

Q8 *earning*

Q9 *with*

Q10 *positions*

Q11 *describing*

Q12 *acclaim*

Test 4 Odd One Out

Q1 *D* *July*

The other three are seasons.

Q2 *D* *sweet*

The other three are prepositions.

Q3 *C* *sadness*

The other three are verbs.

Q4 *B* *license*

The other three are parts of a car.

Q5 *C* *lemon*

The other three are types of berry.

Q6 *C* *relax*

The other three are synonyms.

Q7 *D* *ball*

The other three are sports.

Q8 *A* *leader*

The other three are synonyms.

Q9 *C* *zebra*

The other three are farm animals.

Q10 *B* *grams*

The other three are units that measure distance.

Test 5 Antonyms

Q1 *MINORITY*

Q2 *NEGATIVE*

Q3 *PROBABLE*

Q4 *HINDER*

Q5 *ARTIFICIAL*

Q6 *MISPLACE*

Q7 *ABANDON*

Q8 *WORSE*

Q9 *GENUINE*

Q10 *INNOCENT*

Test 6 Missing Letters

Q1 ACC**OMP**LISH

Q2 DA**MAGE**

Q3 **COM**PONENT

Q4 NA**RR**OW

Q5 AFFLU**ENT**

Q6 DO**NATE**

Q7 IMIT**AT**E

Q8 AUDI**BLE**

Q9 OB**SERVE**

Q10 SEP**ARATE**

Q11 INTI**MATE**

Q12 HIN**DER**

Q13 FOR**TUN**ATE

Q14 **HAR**MLESS

Q15 SATIS**FAC**TORY

Test 7 Correct Sentence

Q1 **A**

There are many ways to solve this problem.

Q2 **D**

The man was always borrowing money from his friend.

Q3 **B**

Many of the hottest countries are close to the equator.

Q4 **C**

You must eat neither wheat nor dairy if you are allergic to them.

Q5 **A**

I asked for the book but he did not lend it to me.

Q6 **D**

Ben ate so many sweets that he felt sick.

Q7 **D**

She is better than me at writing.

Q8 **A**

Paul enjoyed himself on holiday.

Q9 **C**

"Where is my favourite pen?" asked Bob.

Q10 **B**

Whoever works the hardest will win the competition.

Q11 **A**

My father impressed the importance of honesty on me.

Q12 **D**

Always check your bike's brakes before you start riding.

Test 8 Complete the Sentence

Q1 **C** convey

Q2 **A** neglect

Q3 **D** fortune

Q4 **D** prosperity

Q5 **B** bashful

Q6 **E** solitary

Q7 **A** independent

Q8 **B** aroma

Q9 **D** taunted

Q10 **C** obstacles

Test 9 Synonyms

Q1 UNPREDICTABLE

Q2 DOUBTFUL

Q3 RELUCTANT

Q4 TIMID

Q5 ENERGETIC

Q6 DEPENDABLE

Q7 DETERMINED

Q8 PUZZLED

Q9 DELICATE

Q10 OUTRAGED

Test 10 Cloze

Q1 enormous

Q2 proudly

Q3 bubbling

Q4 violent

Q5 uprooted

Q6 tumbled

Q7 addressed

Q8 light

Q9 fight

Q10 contrary

Q11 blows

Q12 flourishing

Test 11 Spelling Mistake

Q1 *E* *abreviate → abbreviate*
Q2 *C* *marinayte → marinate*
Q3 *C* *harbore → harbour*
Q4 *D* *vaypour → vapour*
Q5 *A* *ilusion → illusion*
Q6 *E* *basc → bask*
Q7 *B* *lesiure → leisure*
Q8 *B* *colaborate → collaborate*
Q9 *D* *frantik → frantic*
Q10 *C* *organysed → organised*

Test 12 Change a Letter

Q1 *TABLE*
Q2 *SHOCK*
Q3 *BLEAK*
Q4 *BOLD*
Q5 *PERMIT*
Q6 *EAST*
Q7 *GRADE*
Q8 *SHOUT*
Q9 *POLICY*
Q10 *PAVE*
Q11 *HUNTER*
Q12 *CLARITY*

Test 13 Synonyms

Q1 *D* *scattered*
Q2 *E* *perspire*
Q3 *D* *unhappy*
Q4 *C* *destroy*
Q5 *A* *feisty*
Q6 *C* *distant*
Q7 *D* *change*

Test 14 Fill the Letters

Q1 *ACCURATE*
Q2 *STRANGE*
Q3 *DRAWN*
Q4 *PATTERN*
Q5 *RESEMBLE*

Q6 *DEVELOP*
Q7 *CAPABLE*
Q8 *FRONTIER*
Q9 *SUSTAINABLE*
Q10 *DISCOVER*

Test 15 Cloze

Q1 *roaming*
Q2 *contract*
Q3 *suggesting*
Q4 *sovereign*
Q5 *inhabitants*
Q6 *consented*
Q7 *savage*
Q8 *assistance*
Q9 *vanquished*
Q10 *traitor*
Q11 *blessing*
Q12 *authority*

Test 16 Rearrange the Words

Q1 *There are countless stars in the sky.*
Q2 *The blue car whizzed along the quiet road.*
Q3 *The arsonist fled the scene of his crime.*
Q4 *Several of my colleagues have decided to retire this year.*
Q5 *It's becoming increasingly difficult to justify his actions.*
Q6 *The politician had developed into a formidable adversary.*
Q7 *My watch has stopped working because the battery has run out.*
Q8 *Disease and famine have hindered the country's progress. OR Famine and disease have hindered the country's progress.*

Test 17 Antonyms

Q1 *E* *awkward*
Q2 *A* *disobey*
Q3 *B* *inattentive*
Q4 *C* *unfulfilled*
Q5 *D* *ignore*
Q6 *B* *reasonable*
Q7 *C* *focused*

Test 18 Comprehension

Q1 *A*

Mongoose

Q2 *D*

He was excited about hunting in the garden

Q3 *D*

His child had been devoured by Nag

Q4 *D*

Fearful

Q5 *B*

Scampered

Q6 *C*

Adverb

Test 19 Unnecessary Word

Q1 *D sun*

Correct sentence: The rocky mountains loomed over the grassy field.

Q2 *B soiled*

Correct sentence: Gardeners love to tend to their plants and herbs.

Q3 *B smelled*

Correct sentence: The accountant was shocked by the man's disorganisation.

Q4 *A hoax*

Correct sentence: It is believed that evil spirits dwell inside that house.

Q5 *B fast*

Correct sentence: The forest is slowly disappearing due to illegal logging.

Q6 *C hover*

Correct sentence: The clouds formed a beautiful pattern in the blue sky.

Test 20 Cloze

Q1 *barbarous*

Q2 *Gradually*

Q3 *caves*

Q4 *supply*

Q5 *serviceable*

Q6 *blessing*

Q7 *defence*

Q8 *attained*

Q9 *surrounded*

Q10 *idle*

Q11 *likeness*

Q12 *arrows*

Test 21 Odd One Out

Q1 *B owl*

The other three are sea creatures.

Q2 *C clever*

The other three are synonyms.

Q3 *D television*

The other three are things you read.

Q4 *A hate*

The other three are adjectives.

Q5 *C window*

The other three are things you sit on.

Q6 *B Canada*

The other three are countries in Europe.

Q7 *C reverse*

The other three are synonyms.

Q8 *B cook*

The other three are verbs involving cutting.

Q9 *D lounge*

The other three are synonyms.

Q10 *A garden*

The other three are collective nouns.

Test 22 Antonyms

Q1 *FRESH*

Q2 *ACQUIRE*

Q3 *CONFESS*

Q4 *SOPHISTICATED*

Q5 *TROUGH*

Q6 *INEFFECTIVE*

Q7 *PREDATOR*

Q8 *MULTIPLICATION*

Q9 *ADVANCE*

Q10 *RECKLESS*

Test 23 Missing Letters

Q1 *CARELESSNESS*

Q2 *COMPLIMENT*

Q3	SCAMPER
Q4	MYSTERIOUS
Q5	PESTER
Q6	WONDERFUL
Q7	ACTIVATE
Q8	RELEASE
Q9	BEGINNING
Q10	SURPLUS
Q11	FASCINATING
Q12	OUTGOING
Q13	DISGUISED
Q14	WORTHLESS
Q15	SHOCK

Test 24 Correct Sentence

Q1 **B**

We emerged unharmed from the wreckage.

Q2 **A**

There were several officers here yesterday.

Q3 **D**

There isn't too much I can do to help you.

Q4 **D**

The teacher asked, "How are you all doing today?"

Q5 **A**

The queen's reign lasted seven days.

Q6 **C**

John asked his friend, who was called Fred, to help him.

Q7 **B**

The angry old man shouted at me and my friend.

Q8 **B**

The idle young boy ate all the cookies.

Q9 **A**

The bag was full of apples, bananas and oranges.

Q10 **B**

The man was convicted of stealing the book.

Q11 **A**

Elephants can be found in both Africa and India.

Q12 **D**

The chancellor held up a coloured sheet.

Test 25 Complete the Sentence

Q1	D	excited
Q2	D	impenetrable

Q3	E	endangered
Q4	E	alliance
Q5	B	shocked
Q6	A	scattered
Q7	C	trivial
Q8	C	reckless
Q9	E	escorted
Q10	D	dedicated

Test 26 Synonyms

Q1	OBVIOUS
Q2	UNITED
Q3	INTENTIONAL
Q4	TOWERING
Q5	UNUSUAL
Q6	CORRECT
Q7	DELIGHT
Q8	DISCARD
Q9	WITHDRAW
Q10	ELIMINATE

Test 27 Cloze

Q1	transport
Q2	intensely
Q3	maximum
Q4	paused
Q5	sought
Q6	shadow
Q7	afforded
Q8	claimed
Q9	arose
Q10	maintained
Q11	traveller
Q12	escalated

Test 28 Spelling Mistake

Q1	A	eturnal → eternal
Q2	C	creaiton → creation
Q3	A	dialog → dialogue
Q4	C	plyable → pliable
Q5	B	jear → jeer

Test 28 answers continue on next page

Q6 **C** *wel* → *well*
Q7 **A** *styfle* → *stifle*
Q8 **D** *eazy* → *easy*
Q9 **B** *bizzare* → *bizarre*
Q10 **E** *felow* → *fellow*

Test 29 Change a Letter

Q1 FROST
Q2 HYPE
Q3 WINTER
Q4 FEIGN
Q5 HAWK
Q6 SCARF
Q7 HOVER
Q8 DAIRY
Q9 COMA
Q10 SEVER
Q11 BOTCH
Q12 SLICE

Test 30 Synonyms

Q1 **B** *frugal*
Q2 **A** *thorough*
Q3 **D** *derelict*
Q4 **C** *surround*
Q5 **E** *quick*
Q6 **D** *trustworthy*
Q7 **A** *restricted*

Test 31 Fill the Letters

Q1 ABRUPT
Q2 BOISTEROUS
Q3 MUNDANE
Q4 PROSPEROUS
Q5 INTREPID
Q6 CONTROVERSY
Q7 STRATEGY
Q8 CALAMITY
Q9 DESTITUTE
Q10 REPLENISH

Test 32 Cloze

Q1 *forced*
Q2 *gnawing*
Q3 *ravaged*
Q4 *abandoned*
Q5 *desecrated*
Q6 *wandered*
Q7 *insolent*
Q8 *rounded*
Q9 *destructive*
Q10 *expel*
Q11 *encounter*
Q12 *stupor*

Test 33 Rearrange the Words

Q1 *The department store was struggling to attract shoppers.*
Q2 *The new policy will not come into effect until next year.*
Q3 *We would like to offer you a complimentary beverage.*
Q4 *The arrogant lawyer dismissed my valid concerns.*
Q5 *The king decided to endorse neither candidate.*
Q6 *The rhinoceros lowered his head to drink from the stream.*
Q7 *My mother was a very perceptive woman.*
Q8 *The toddlers were captivated by the magical clown.*

Test 34 Antonyms

Q1 **A** *crooked*
Q2 **B** *hostile*
Q3 **E** *accept*
Q4 **B** *detest*
Q5 **D** *comforting*
Q6 **D** *brisk*
Q7 **E** *comical*

Test 35 Comprehension

Q1 **B**
        March

Q2 **E**
        Symbolic

Q3 *E*

Five

Q4 *A*

Entertained

Q5 *B*

Planned

Q6 *C*

He feared for his safety

Test 36 Unnecessary Word

Q1 *B fragrant*

Correct sentence: The loyal supporters attended every match.

Q2 *A biased*

Correct sentence: The boy was not sure of the correct answer.

Q3 *A admiringly*

Correct sentence: The young teacher confidently challenged her seniors. OR The young teacher challenged her seniors confidently.

Q4 *D stoning*

Correct sentence: There are significant obstacles in the path ahead.

Q5 *D seven*

Correct sentence: The two scenarios were both troubling for the company.

Q6 *B it*

Correct sentence: The scholars found the translation to be inaccurate.

Test 37 Cloze

Q1 struck

Q2 damage

Q3 demolished

Q4 dwellings

Q5 attending

Q6 unable

Q7 collapsed

Q8 worshippers

Q9 indicates

Q10 boundaries

Q11 generated

Q12 waves

Test 38 Odd One Out

Q1 *C arm*

The other three are joints.

Q2 *B leaf*

The other three are types of tree.

Q3 *B man*

The other three are types of relations.

Q4 *A sometimes*

The other three are synonyms.

Q5 *B painting*

The other three are tools used to create a painting.

Q6 *D cucumber*

The other three are red in colour.

Q7 *B snake*

The other three are mammals.

Q8 *D deceitful*

The other three are synonyms.

Q9 *A forge*

The other three are occupations.

Q10 *C ocean*

The other three are found on land.

Test 39 Antonyms

Q1 COMPLICATE

Q2 HEALTHY

Q3 TRUSTING

Q4 PLEASANT

Q5 SQUANDER

Q6 SUBTLE

Q7 MINUTE

Q8 INARTICULATE

Q9 POLITE

Q10 ADVANCE

Test 40 Missing Letters

Q1 ENTHUSIASTIC

Q2 FLEXIBLE

Q3 AUTHORISE

Q4 EXPOSE

Q5 SURRENDER

Q6 OBTAINABLE

Test 40 answers continue on next page

Q7 INVALIDATE

Q8 CELEBRATE

Q9 ENVELOP

Q10 ANIMATED

Q11 CHANGEABLE

Q12 INDIFFERENT

Q13 ERRONEOUS

Q14 UNREASONABLE

Q15 FRAGRANT

Test 41 Correct Sentence

Q1 *A*

Warm clothing is essential for this voyage.

Q2 *D*

I forgave him for betraying me.

Q3 *C*

You need to apply for some work experience.

Q4 *A*

Linda drew seven fish and three sheep on the paper.

Q5 *C*

Pollution of the environment is a global issue.

Q6 *B*

The courageous girl swiftly defeated the dragon.

Q7 *A*

Please don't forget to pick up your litter.

Q8 *C*

All except one of the caterpillars transformed into butterflies.

Q9 *D*

"There was no choice!" yelled the instructor.

Q10 *A*

The astronaut, who had trained for many years, was selected to go into space.

Q11 *A*

All the children participated in the event.

Q12 *C*

It's warmer in summer than in winter.

Test 42 Complete the Sentence

Q1 *B* flawed

Q2 *D* fast

Q3 *E* upheld

Q4 *B* manual

Q5 *D* predominantly

Q6 *E* lack

Q7 *A* diligently

Q8 *B* cease

Q9 *D* negotiator

Q10 *B* yearned

Test 43 Synonyms

Q1 EXCITE

Q2 WISE

Q3 UNOCCUPIED

Q4 INUNDATE

Q5 SUBTRACTION

Q6 MALEVOLENT

Q7 DISCLOSE

Q8 BANISH

Q9 CHEERFUL

Q10 OVERCAST

Test 44 Cloze

Q1 youth

Q2 yielded

Q3 encountered

Q4 seized

Q5 rotten

Q6 master

Q7 extremely

Q8 fault

Q9 spirit

Q10 infirmities

Q11 praised

Q12 blamed

Test 45 Spelling Mistake

Q1 *B* rewthless ➜ ruthless

Q2 *D* synical ➜ cynical

Q3 *A* colourfull ➜ colourful

Q4 *E* plouw ➜ plough

Q5 *C* arogance ➜ arrogance

Q6 *D* repetiton ➜ repetition

Q7 *E* intrust ➜ entrust

Q8 **D** *asail → assail*

Q9 **C** *lazyness → laziness*

Q10 **B** *conseal → conceal*

Test 46 Change a Letter

Q1 SMART

Q2 HEED

Q3 REFINE

Q4 ATTACH

Q5 SAVOUR

Q6 CRUISE

Q7 SHEAR

Q8 FAWN

Q9 SHALLOW

Q10 TASTE

Q11 CLAMOUR

Q12 WALLOW

Test 47 Synonyms

Q1 **E** *reduce*

Q2 **B** *outstanding*

Q3 **E** *produce*

Q4 **C** *frustrate*

Q5 **E** *brusque*

Q6 **C** *combine*

Q7 **B** *drain*

Test 48 Fill the Letters

Q1 AMPLE

Q2 RUBBISH

Q3 ENDEARING

Q4 OMNIVORE

Q5 SERENE

Q6 CULPABLE

Q7 ASPIRE

Q8 PLACATE

Q9 DIVULGE

Q10 RECTIFY

Test 49 Cloze

Q1 *primarily*

Q2 *discoveries*

Q3 *notation*

Q4 *worldwide*

Q5 *areas*

Q6 *ancient*

Q7 *widespread*

Q8 *deductive*

Q9 *contributions*

Q10 *throughout*

Q11 *millennium*

Q12 *transmitted*

Test 50 Rearrange the Words

Q1 *The new facility will be used to conduct experiments.*

Q2 *Many people in the world still live in great poverty.*

Q3 *The determined army marched across the battlefield.*

Q4 *The gardener planted some seeds in his allotment.*

Q5 *Please do not proceed beyond this point.*

Q6 *The manager set impossible goals for his team.*

Q7 *His new proposal was met with unanimous approval.*

Q8 *My damp clothes were left outside to dry.*

Test 51 Antonyms

Q1 **D** *ignore*

Q2 **A** *antidote*

Q3 **E** *careless*

Q4 **E** *common*

Q5 **B** *inept*

Q6 **A** *scatter*

Q7 **C** *dismantle*

Test 52 Comprehension

Q1 **B**

Tugged

Q2 **E**

It was a ship that could fly

Test 52 answers continue on next page

Q3 **B**
Relaxed

Q4 **C**
Because it was destroyed

Q5 **D**
He could throw boulders the size of pickup trucks

Q6 **A**
Fiction

Test 53 Unnecessary Word

Q1 **C** *having*

Correct sentence: You must remember to brush your teeth.

Q2 **D** *growth*

Correct sentence: The two wrestlers did not respect one another.

Q3 **A** *instrument*

Correct sentence: The nurse loved to play music in the evening.

Q4 **B** *coined*

Correct sentence: The banker fell for the forger's ruse.

Q5 **C** *tusk*

Correct sentence: Elephants are very caring and considerate. OR Elephants are very considerate and caring.

Q6 **D** *salt*

Correct sentence: The setting sun disappeared over the horizon.

Test 54 Spelling Mistake

Q1 **E** *justise* → *justice*
Q2 **A** *heroizm* → *heroism*
Q3 **D** *bussiness* → *business*
Q4 **B** *comission* → *commission*
Q5 **C** *percieve* → *perceive*
Q6 **E** *lettice* → *lettuce*
Q7 **B** *proklaim* → *proclaim*
Q8 **D** *medle* → *meddle*
Q9 **A** *oposite* → *opposite*
Q10 **E** *iritate* → *irritate*

Test 55 Change a Letter

Q1 CAPE
Q2 AVERT

Q3 COVER
Q4 PESTER
Q5 GROUND
Q6 HERB
Q7 YEARN
Q8 CRACKED
Q9 SWINDLE
Q10 SHIVER
Q11 HAZY
Q12 CATER

Notes

Notes

ACKNOWLEDGEMENTS

The author and publisher are grateful to the copyright holders for permission to use quoted materials and images.

Cover & P.1 © Lee Yiu Tung/Shutterstock.com; P.4 *Charlie and the Chocolate Factory* by Roald Dahl, reproduced by permission of David Higham Associates Limited; P.44 From *One Summer* by Bill Bryson, published by Doubleday. Reprinted by permission of The Random House Group Ltd; P.64 *The House of Hades* by Rick Riordan (Puffin Books 2013) © Rick Riordan 2013, reproduced by permission of Penguin Books Ltd.

Every effort has been made to trace copyright holders and obtain their permission for the use of copyright material. The author and publisher will gladly receive information enabling them to rectify any error or omission in subsequent editions. All facts are correct at time of going to press.

Published by Letts Educational

An imprint of HarperCollins*Publishers* Limited
1 London Bridge Street
London SE1 9GF

ISBN: 9781844198917

First published 2017

10 9 8 7 6 5 4 3 2 1

© HarperCollins*Publishers* Limited

British Library Cataloguing in Publication Data.

A CIP record of this book is available from the British Library.

Author: Faisal Nasim

Commissioning Editor: Michelle I'Anson

Editor and Project Manager: Sonia Dawkins

Cover Design: Paul Oates and Sarah Duxbury

Text Design, Layout and Artwork: Q2A Media

Production: Paul Harding

Printed by RR Donnelley APS

Please note that Letts is not associated with CEM or The University of Durham in any way. This book does not contain any official questions and it is not endorsed by CEM or The University of Durham.

Our question types are based on those set by CEM, but we cannot guarantee that your child's actual 11+ exam will contain the same question types or format as this book.

CEM, Centre for Evaluation and Monitoring and *The University of Durham* are all trademarks of The University of Durham.